Fossils

Andrea Rivera

abdopublishing.com

Published by Abdo Zoom™, PO Box 398166, Minneapolis, Minnesota 55439. Copyright © 2018 by
Abdo Consulting Group, Inc. International copyrights reserved in all countries. No part of this book may be
reproduced in any form without written permission from the publisher. Abdo Zoom™ is a trademark and logo
of Abdo Consulting Group, Inc.

Printed in the United States of America, North Mankato, Minnesota
012017
092017

**THIS BOOK CONTAINS
RECYCLED MATERIALS**

Cover Photo: Shutterstock Images
Interior Photos: Shutterstock Images, 1, 4–5, 6, 7, 8–9, 9, 13, 14, 16–17, 19; Marcio Jose Bastos Silva/
Shutterstock Images, 5; Reynold Sumayku/Alamy, 11; Geologist Natural Pics/Shutterstock Images, 12;
Vyacheslav Svetlichnyy/Shutterstock Images, 15; Audrius Merfeldas/Shutterstock Images, 17; Lee Prince/
Shutterstock Images, 18; Michal Ninger/Shutterstock Images, 21

Editor: Emily Temple
Series Designer: Madeline Berger
Art Direction: Dorothy Toth

Publisher's Cataloging-in-Publication Data
Names: Rivera, Andrea, author.
Title: Fossils / by Andrea Rivera.
Description: Minneapolis, MN : Abdo Zoom, 2018. | Series: Rocks and minerals |
    Includes bibliographical references and index.
Identifiers: LCCN 2017930332 | ISBN 9781532120435 (lib. bdg.) |
    ISBN 9781614797548 (ebook) | ISBN 9781614798101 (Read-to-me ebook)
Subjects: LCSH: Fossils--Juvenile literature.
Classification: DDC 560--dc23
LC record available at http://lccn.loc.gov/2017930332

Table of Contents

Science

Fossils form over many years. They **preserve** signs of life. There are two kinds of fossils.

4

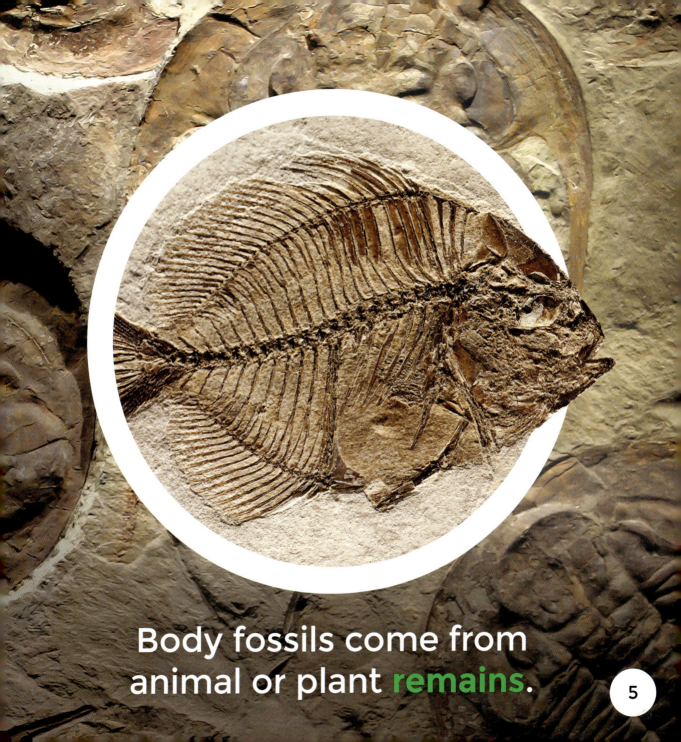

Body fossils come from animal or plant **remains**.

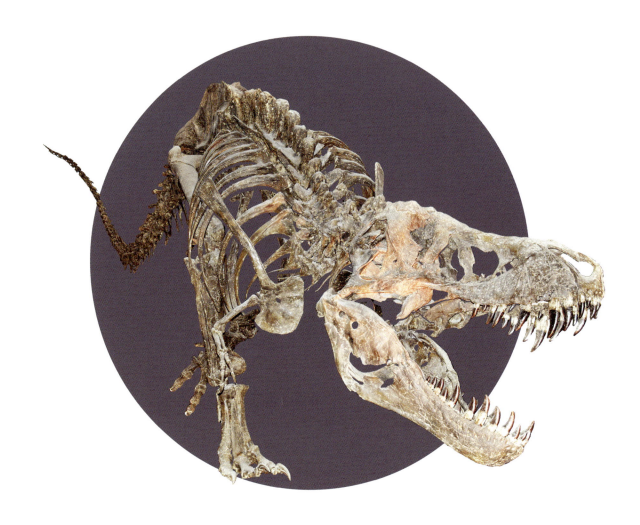

Soil covers the remains. It pushes down on them. The soil turns to rock. This forms a fossil.

Some body fossils are millions of years old.

Trace fossils show where a living thing has been. A footprint can become a trace fossil. The footprint is covered by **sediment**.

It hardens into rock.

Technology

Fossils are often found in the ground. Scientists search for them. Sometimes they use **radar**. This helps them see what is underground.

Fossils break easily.
Scientists work in small areas.
They remove the fossils slowly.

Special tools help
them be gentle.

Engineering

Coal is a **fossil fuel**. It is made from dead plants. People dig coal from deep underground.

Coal can be burned to heat buildings. It can also be used to make electricity.

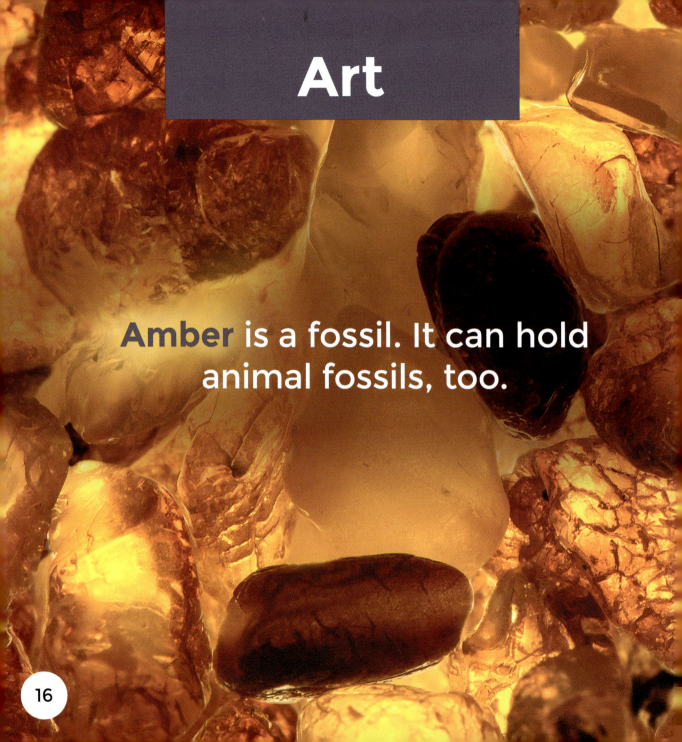

Art

Amber is a fossil. It can hold animal fossils, too.

16

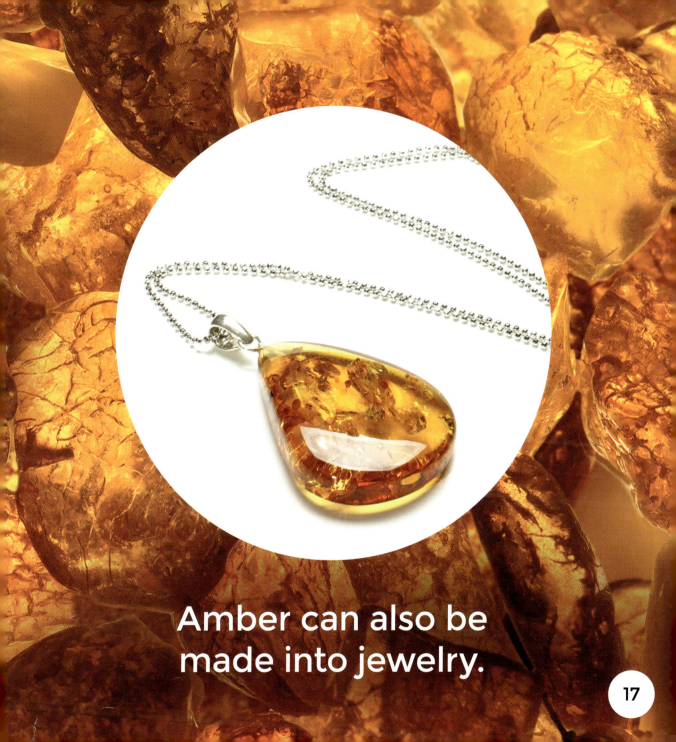

Amber can also be
made into jewelry.

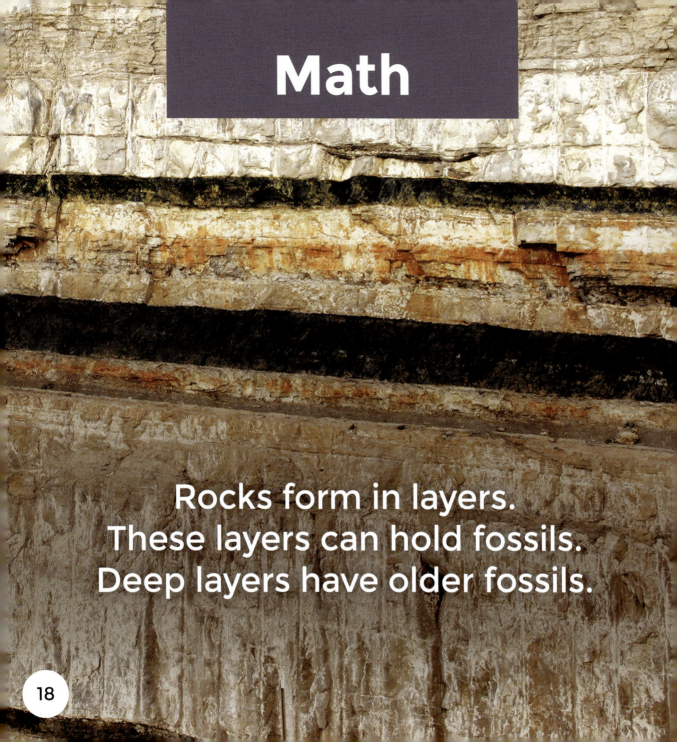

Math

Rocks form in layers.
These layers can hold fossils.
Deep layers have older fossils.

Fossils helped scientists determine Earth's age. It is likely 3.5 to 3.8 billion years old.

Key Stats

- Scientists compare old fossils to new ones. They learn about Earth's history.

- The oldest known fossil is 3.5 billion years old.

- Not all animals or plants become fossils. An animal or plant must die in a place where mud, sand, or soil can easily cover the body. Once covered, the body is protected. Time passes. It becomes a fossil.

Glossary

amber - a hard substance that forms from fossilized plants.

fossil fuel - a material formed from dead plants or animals that produces power when burned.

preserve - keep safe or maintain.

radar - a way to find objects by bouncing radio waves off them.

remains - what is left of the body after an animal or plant dies.

sediment - pieces of solid material such as minerals, rocks, or sand.

Booklinks

For more information on fossils, please visit abdobooklinks.com

 In on STEAM!

Learn even more with the Abdo Zoom STEAM database. Check out abdozoom.com for more information.

Index